THE BEAUTY OF GOD'S WORD

PHOTOS BY I. GOLD

The Beauty of God's Word

The text of this book was based on the public domain version of the JPS translation of the Tanakh.

DEDICATION

This book is dedicated to my brother who gave me the tools to be a better photographer and the example to be a better person.

And in loving memory of my father, grandparents, and all those family members who have gone before.

ACKNOWLEDGEMENTS

With special thanks to my mother, my sister, brother-in-law, sister-in-law, nieces, nephews, cousins – I love you all.

To my friends, too numerous to mention, thank you for being a part of my life.

Lift up your eyes on high and see
Who has created these!

Isaiah 40:26

Open my eyes that I may behold
wondrous things out of your law.
Psalm 119:18

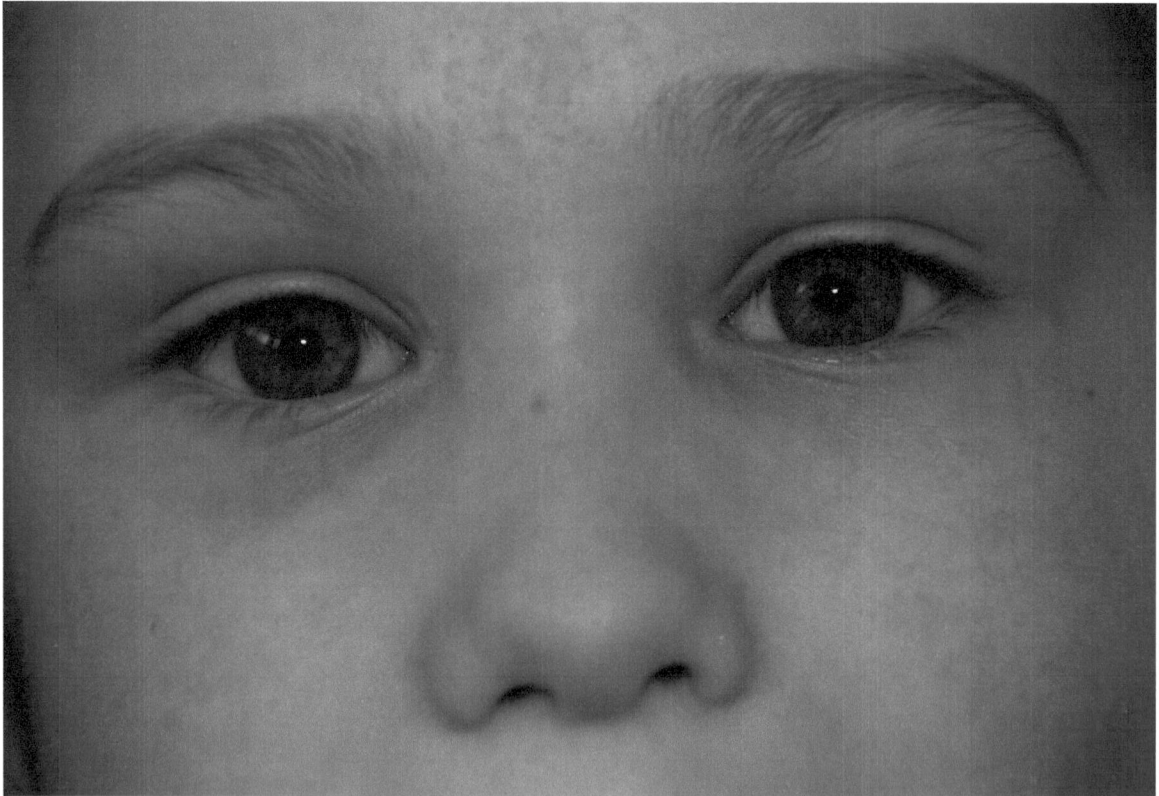

Your word is a lamp to my feet and a light to my path.
Psalm 119:105

But the path of the righteous is as the light of dawn, that shines more and more unto the perfect day.
Proverbs 4:18

By the breath of God ice is given…
Job 37:10

He satisfies your old age with good things
so that your youth is renewed like the eagle.
Psalm 103:5

And the light is sweet and a pleasant thing it is for the eyes to behold the sun.
Ecclesiastes 11:7

You open your hand and satisfy every living thing with favor.
Psalm 145:16

You are the Lord...who has made heaven...the earth...the seas and all that is in them.
Nehemiah 9:6

Above the noises of many waters, the mighty breakers of the sea, the Lord on high is mighty.
Psalm 93:4

And God said: "Let the earth bring forth the living creature after its kind…"
Genesis 1:24

I have blotted out, as a thick cloud, your transgressions, and as a cloud, your sins; return unto Me, for I have redeemed you.
Isaiah 44:22

He makes me to lie down in green pastures. He leads me besides the still waters. He restores my soul.
Psalm 23:2,3

He only is my rock and my salvation...
I shall not be moved.
Psalm 62:7

Your loving kindness, O Lord, is in the heavens; Your faithfulness reaches unto the skies.
Psalm 36:6

Remember the word which Moses...commanded you, saying: The Lord your God gives you rest and will give you this land.

Joshua 1:13

For you light my lamp; The Lord my God
lightens my darkness.
Psalm 18:29

Your hands have made me and fashioned me...
Psalm 119:73

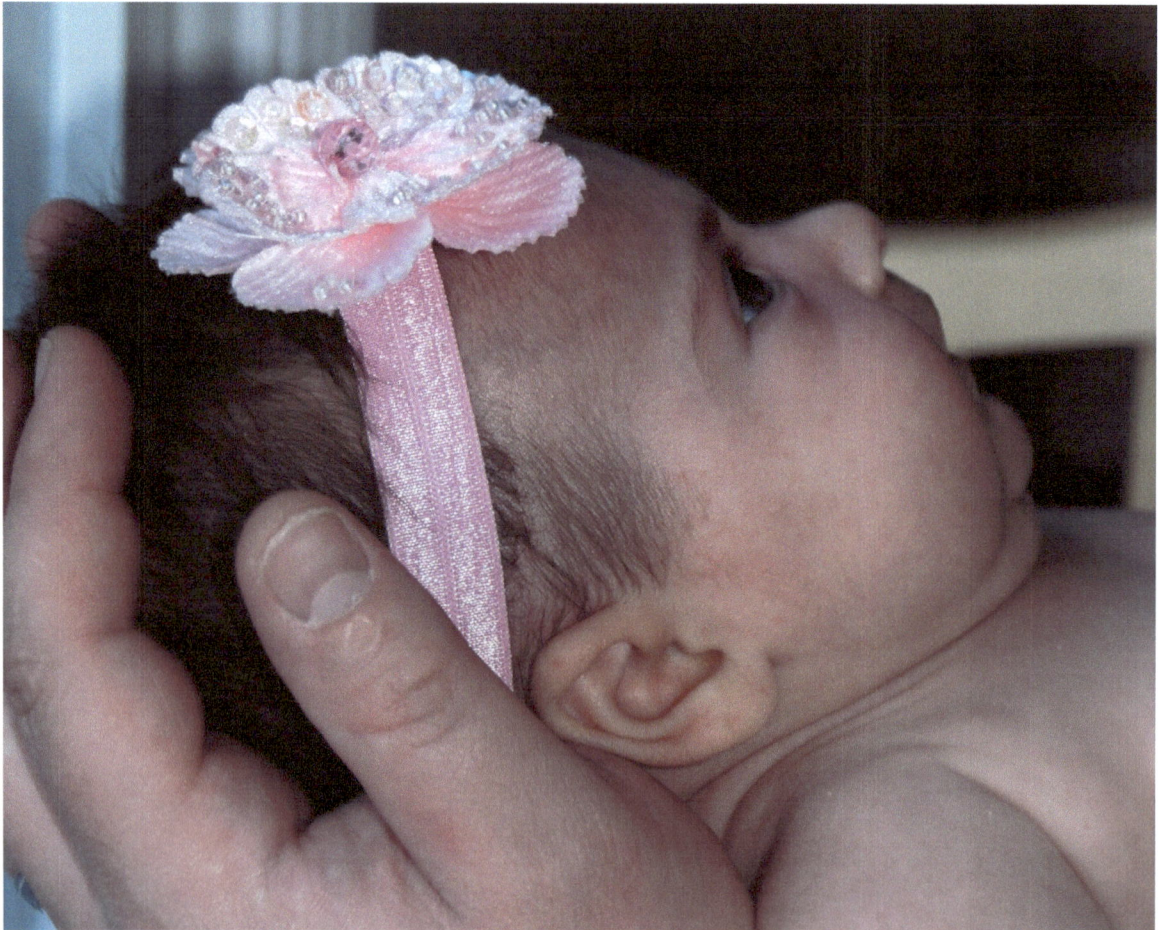

In all your ways acknowledge Him, and
He will direct your paths.
Proverbs 3:6

I will lift up my eyes unto the mountains: from where shall my help come? My help comes from the Lord, who made heaven and earth.
Psalm 121: 1,2

The heavens declare the glory of God, and
the firmament shows His handiwork.
Psalm 19:1

The flowers appear on the earth; the time of singing is come…
Song of Songs 2:12

For a thousand years in Your sight are but as yesterday…
Psalm 90:4

Let be, and know that I am God...
Psalm 46:11

I will be as the dew unto Israel...
Hosea 14:6

He spoke unto them in the pillar of cloud;
they kept His testimonies, and the statute
that He gave them.
Psalm 99:7

Then shall the trees of the wood sing with joy before the Lord...
1 Chronicles 16:33

For you shall go out with joy, and be led forth with peace; the mountains and the hills shall break forth before you into singing, and the trees of the field shall clap their hands.

Isaiah 55:12

...His voice was like the sound of many waters, and the earth did shine with His glory.
Ezekiel 43:2

Only for God does my soul wait in stillness. From him comes my salvation.
Psalm 62:2

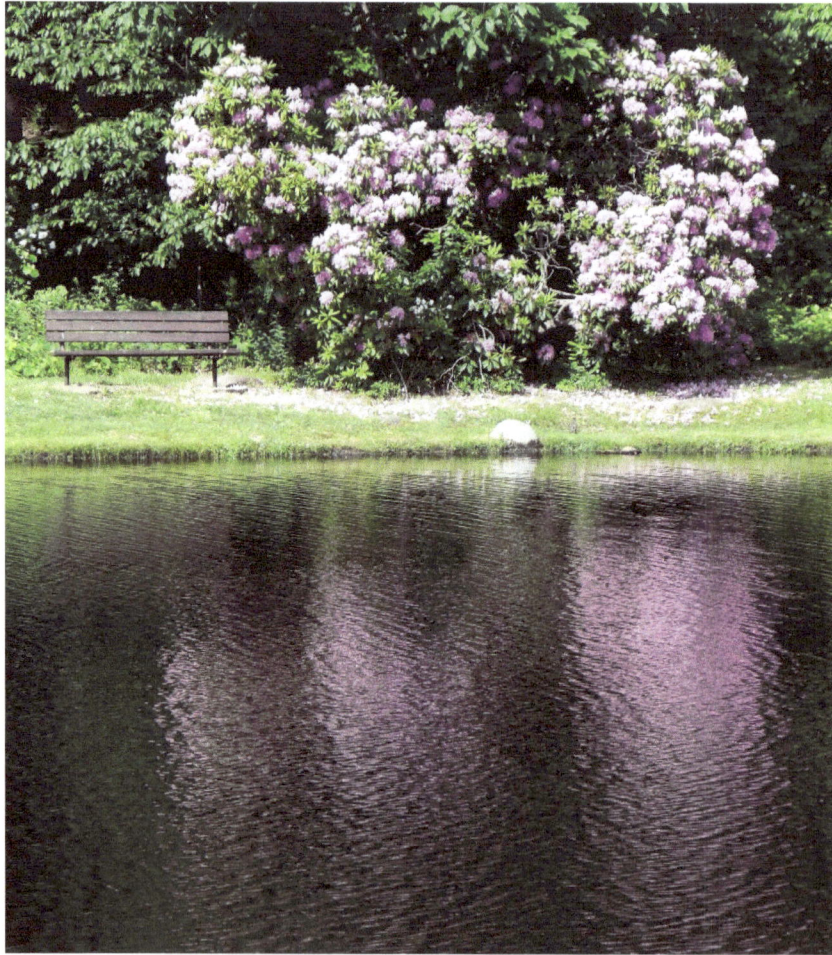

Wash me thoroughly from my iniquity
and cleanse me from my sin...wash me,
and I shall be whiter than snow.
Psalm 51:4,9

He will cover you with His wings, and under His wings you shall take refuge.
Psalm 91:4

He has made every living thing beautiful
in its time...
Ecclesiastes 3:11

But ask the fowls of the air, and they shall tell you...in whose hand is the soul of every living thing and the breath of all mankind.
Job 12:7,10

Arise, shine, for your light is come, and
the glory of the Lord is risen upon you.
Isaiah 60:1

Him that darkens day into night; that calls for the waters of the sea, and pours them out upon the face of the earth; the Lord is his name.

Amos 5:8

Blessed is the man that trusts in the Lord...For he shall be as a tree planted by the waters, and that spreads out its roots by the brook.
Jeremiah 17:7,8

All the fowls of heaven made their nests in its boughs, and all the beasts of the field did bring forth their young under its branches.
Ezekiel 31:6

...and by His light, I walked through darkness.
Job 29:3

This is the Lord's doing; it is marvelous in
our eyes.
Psalm 118:23

In blessing I will bless you, and in multiplying, I will multiply your seed...as the sand which is on the seashore.
Genesis 22:17

So shall you delight yourself in the Lord; and he shall give you the petitions of your heart.
Psalm 37:4

For as the earth brings forth her growth, and as the garden causes the things that are sown in it to spring forth; so the Lord God will cause victory and glory to spring forth before all the nations.
Isaiah 61:11

Pleasant words are as honey, sweet to the soul and health to the bones.
Proverbs 16:24

For you have been my help, and in the shadow of Your wings, do I rejoice.
Psalm 63:8

I form the light and create darkness;...
I am the Lord that does all these things.
Isaiah 45:7

His anger is but for a moment, His favor is for a lifetime. Weeping may stay for the night, but joy comes in the morning.
Psalm 30:6

The wilderness and the parched land
shall be glad; and the desert shall rejoice
and blossom as the flower.
Isaiah 35:1

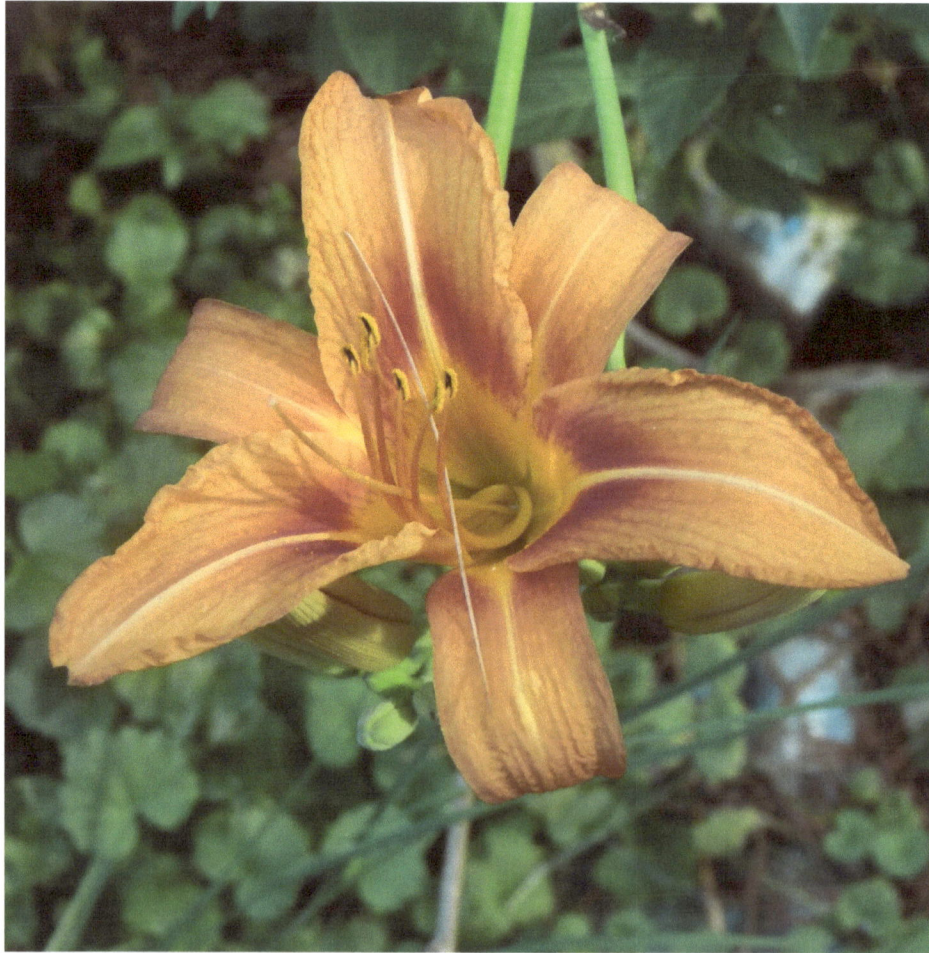

Sing to the Lord with thanksgiving;
sing praises upon the harp to our God.
Psalm 147:7

As one whom his mother comforts,
so will I comfort you.
Isaiah 66:13

The Lord is your keeper, the Lord is your shade at your right hand. The sun shall not smite you by day, nor the moon by night. The Lord will keep you from all evil; He shall keep your soul.
Psalm 121 5-7

From the rising of the sun to its going down, the Lord's name is to be praised.
Psalm 113:3

www.ingramcontent.com/pod-product-compliance
Lightning Source LLC
LaVergne TN
LVHW072052070426
835508LV00002B/61